THE BOOK OF SPLENDOR:
NEW AND SELECTED POEMS ON
SPIRITUAL THEMES

THE BOOK OF SPLENDOR: NEW AND SELECTED POEMS ON SPIRITUAL THEMES

Poems by

David Shaddock

Cover design by Shay Culligan
Cover art by Terry Braunstein

ISBN: 978-1-949229-92-9

Kelsay Books Inc.

kelsaybooks.com

502 S 1040 E, A119
American Fork, Utah 84003

By David Shaddock

Poetry:

Dreams Are Another Set of Muscles
In This Place Where Something's Missing *Lives*
Vernal Pool

Non-fiction:

From Impasse to Intimacy
Contexts and Connections
Poetry and Psychoanalysis: The Opening of the Field (forthcoming)

For my teachers
Denise Levertov and Rabbi Burt Jacobson

Acknowledgments

"For the Dyings" is from *Dreams Are Another Set of Muscles.* In Between Books, 1987

In This Place Where Something's Missing *Lives* was published in a letterpress edition in by Alileah Press, NYC., 1991

"Shabbes Eve," "Walk" and "After Psalm 23," are from *Vernal Pool,* White Violet Press, 2015.

Poems in this manuscript appeared in *Tikkun, The J Weekly, By the Well of Living Waters, The Cistercian Quarterly, International Journal of Psychoanalytic Self Psychology, Panjandrum Review, Yefief, Bosque, Earth First! Journal,*

Sections VII and XI of *In This Place Where* Something's Missing *Lives* were included in the essay "Some Affinities of Content" by Denise Levertov, (*New and Selected Essays,* New Directions, 1992).

Many thanks to Denise Levertov, Anita Barrows, Susan Glickman Dawn McGuire, Peter Dale Scott, Alan Williamson, Jeanne Foster, Phyllis Stowell, Sandra Gilbert, Beverly Brahic, Murray Silverstien, Steve Kowit and Emily Warn for their comments and suggestions over the years.

The sonnets included in this collection employ a hendecasyllabic form that was suggested to me by John Oliver Simon.

Foreword

If you hold, along with Wallace Stevens, that "God and the imagination are one" the distinction between spiritual and secular poetry largely dissolves. As my teacher and friend Denise Levertov maintained, all poetry, by virtue of its very existence, is spiritual. "Shook foil," says Hopkins, and the world shimmers anew with God's Grandeur. But no more so, I would maintain, than in a poem denouncing injustice, or describing a moment's peace or a moment in a personal hell.

Nonetheless the category of spiritual poetry appeals to me, if only to rescue poems that document our struggles with faith, our joys and despairs, from a group of "spiritual" poems where the only emotion allowed is a kind of self-congratulatory awe. Our western notion of faith derives from Jacob's nightlong wrestle with the angel of god, which ends in a draw, save for a sexual-seeming wound and a new name.

The fourth section of this collection, In This Place Where *Something's Missing* Lives, documents a time some thirty years ago of god-wrestling in my own life; a time in which my mother was killed by a medical error and my wife and I were struggling with infertility. Out of these twin difficulties I began to see that our struggles with faith—along with our longing for a connection with something divine—constitute *in themselves* a legitimate faith life.

That God inhabits the space in which we long for Him has become the basis for my subsequent spiritual life. The teachings of the Hasidic masters, referenced in many of the epigraphs to the poem, were a central inspiration in the writing. In that long poem of many sections (as well as in "Splendor," the similarly-structured poem that concludes this collection), I proceed by letting myself associate to the imagery and wisdom in a specific line or passage. The poet Robert Duncan is a major influence here.

The permission to develop a passionate, if idiosyncratic, relationship to texts and traditions was further nurtured by two wise and compassionate teachers, Denise Levertov and Rabbi Burt Jacobson. Denise was in the process of converting from a kind of diffuse spirituality—based in the twin inheritances of her father's Hasidism and her mother's Welch mysticism—to a life as a devout Catholic. This spiritual awakening--which I shared with her through the poems she showed me and in many a long night of conversation—awakened in me a parallel interest and renewed commitment to my long-simmering Jewish faith.

In the same years of the 1980's, Rabbi Burt Jacobson was helping to initiate a new wave of Jewish religiosity which eventually took the name of Jewish Renewal. His vision, along with a number of fellow rabbis, was to link a sense of Hasidic-informed Judaism of participation, joy and passion with a spiritually based commitment to peace, justice and the survival of the planet.

In putting this collection together I have tried, at least thematically, to map my spiritual development. I begin with poems of nature, my first and most constant source of inspiration. The Tell collects poems of longing and realization. These poems mine Jewish sources: the practice of Shabbat, the Book of Psalms, the teachings of Hasidism and Kabbalah. But they mine Christian and Buddhist sources as well. Part III, A Great Blue Heron in Boynton Beach, sees these themes increasingly tinged with the sense of mortality and the threat to the planet. The last section, the long poem "Splendor," derives from a reading of Daniel Matt's translation of the Zohar, "the book of splendor," the central book of Kabbalah and Jewish mysticism. A central tenet of Jewish mysticism is the idea that the world itself is a husk hiding sparks of the divine. "Splendor" marks my attempts as a poet to find these sparks in our everyday life.

In a world where the divide between the self-professed religious and the defensive (or at times offensive) non-believer seems to be inexorably growing, it is my hope that these poems offer a third way, a way in which doubt exists as an essential part of faith and our transitory moments of deep spiritual comfort live in the context of everyday grief and the grief we feel for our beloved planet.

David Shaddock

Contents

IV IN THIS PLACE WHERE *SOMETHING'S MISSING* LIVES

V SPLENDOR

I

LIGHT ON GRANITE

Light on Granite

The granite boulder
backlit at sunrise

seams to float
on blue and gold light.

A water ouzel sings
from his nest by the inlet.

Your just-opened eyes
ring the world like a bell.

On the Kings Kern Divide

The air so dry at 13,000 feet
you feel stretched out
the shadow on the scree
your actual size.
Fields of lupine
so vast across the cirque

you first mistake them
for a chain of lakes.
Mica flecked granite
broken cones of Jeffrey pines
a single, sharp raptor call
as if from inside your skull.

November, Tilden

Horsetail rushes by the soggy trail.
Ear fungi perch on fragile redwood deadfalls.
Damp from the tips
of new sprung grasses
soaks my sneakers
clings to the pores of my sweatshirt.

What is it that holds us?
Nothing suggests the slow
persistent rain; we're all
sloughing off toward Wildcat
Creek, San Pablo Bay
and on the ebb tide, the sea.

Egret, Albany Marsh

Strobed by headlights
each pose is stopped in time
like a silver gelatin print:

white tufted head turned sideways
long neck arched over brackish water
thin legs splayed to dip or feed.

You startle as the startled bird lifts
off the mudflats and wheels
out over the Bay

leaving only a crescent of moon
blinking bridgelights
and a trace of white.

Carmel Valley

1.

The sea breeze driven crowns
of live oaks roll
up the valley like waves.
The hair on my arms
would like to join them.

2.

First LSD trip, Pfeiffer Beach
south of here, I thought
that's all we are
crest and trough, crest
and trough.

3.

My friend Chad spends his days
in chest waders, counting
red legged frogs, looking
for steelhead, restoring
the riparian canopy.

4.

A hawk tracks the contours
of the canyon lip
soaring the rising thermals.
Red tailed? Cooper's? I knew
once, or thought I did.

21

Viewpoint

It's easy to imagine the lost world
of the Ohlone when the fog covers all
but the tip of Tamalpais.
Riparian groves of cottonwood and laurel
redwood on the shaded hillsides
acres of oakflat and bunchgrass
wetlands filled with a hundred species of birds.
Salmon in the creeks, cormorants
streaking the horizon, nothing
taken without return.
My mother and father not dead
but with me now, in the hills
in the wind, a wheel of ancestors
and future descendants
turning like circumpolar stars
around the center of creation
which is a point in my chest
two fingers above the heart.

North Fork of the Tuolumne River

Below a four-foot cascade
the turbulent white river
makes two more falls
then slows into a riffle

where the froth is broken
by random patches of lucent water
tinged gold by the mica flecked
granite the still pools reveal.

Do we have another life?
I've noticed, when grief
becomes unbearable, a sense
of narcotic peace emerges

as if kindness were
a first principle of the universe.
The westward curling river
hits a snag of deadfall

trees, foams up
and leaps into a series
of sharp cascades
down the canyon.

Alhambra Creek

Foxtails wave on the dry hills, contours supple
Like hips and buttocks running in a line up
From Carquinez strait, while laurel and cottonwood
Tangles mark the dense valley bottom's thick green

Promise of year-round water John Muir tapped
For Martinez orchards. Forty years ago
I thought the wavy contour lines that run up
The hillsides were hallucination, showing

The truth that matter was made of waves. Later
I saw that it was the cattle tracks from years
Of lateral grazing. Meat and Metta—clash

Of two realities I've never reconciled.
And now, nearing seventy, may never.
The milk thistle's purple flower, crowning spikes.

II

THE TELL

Hornet

A gray and black hornet
longer than the word *hornet*
typed in 12 point on my computer screen
keeps whacking at the window
ignoring the open pane nearby.
I could squash it with *Couples*
Therapy with Trauma Survivors
which, though a paperback
has plenty of heft for the job.
But some admixture of fear
and kindness has me looking
in a drawer for something
it might walk onto. What I find
is a postcard from the Art Institute
commemorating the loan
of Caravaggio's *Supper at Emmaus.*
The hornet walks its almost translucent legs
onto the head of Saint Luke
for the short trip to the window
and freedom, which seems
to surprise it. I keep
moving my eyes back and forth
from the subtly glowing Christ
to the illuminated face
of the astonished Apostle.

Religion

I've decided to be a little bit of everything.
I see the kind presence of the Virgin everywhere
in the swaying of the cypress in the roadside windbreak
in the busy mom carrying her son's violin case into school.
I let each breath erase memory and expectation
and take me to the door of the Pure Blue Land.
Friend, you're drunk I tell myself
bowing and swirling and kissing the wind.
I was a danger to my own son
when suddenly an angel stayed my hand.
Now turn to your neighbor and say
"behold the face of the Lord."
Will you come with me, beloved
here where the first buds of yellow grass flowers
appear on the hillside?
What amazes me is that Dodge Ram pickups
and bighorn sheep all emerge from the chaos
a single word ordered.
See now in the dew-filled dawn how the yearling
fawn effortlessly leaps the fenceline.
Christ the Essene was sent here to help me.

At Costco

I'm in the parking lot trying to balance
A four foot tall shrinkwrapped package of toilet
Paper. An oblique glance reveals the sunset
Reflected in the still lee of the dog park

At Point Isabel, sandwich wrappers against
The chain link, mottled clouds on the shoulder of
Tamalpais. Golden retrievers splash
After arcing tennis balls. Air-wrenches whine

On lugnuts; Kanye blasts from the Duster, thanks
For sharing. With my fob in one hand I am
Trying to unlatch the hatchback and not spill

My smoothie. Is this the second space Milosz
Saw, *the unattainable small valley?*
Last light on the blue-roofed bulk mail terminal.

After Psalm 65: *For You Silence Is Praise*

I need to get out of my own way, too clever
By a half, and find the praise that speaks itself.
The silence that praises YaH is the song gnarled
Live oaks sing, the rhyolite thrust of Indian

Rock, the last light past Albany Hill over
Brooks Island. It is the settle after cars
Pass, the music (George Benson, On Broadway) still
Playing as the janitor cleans the hallway.

A landscape of prisons we've built, Pelican
Bay to Chowchilla, Vacaville, San Quentin
Chino, the shit reeking Harris Ranch feedlot.

But You still receive our prayer, the first stars
Over the Bay, red blinking microwave
Towers, all silent at their core, praising You.

Shabbat

Leave off the work
of building
and remembering.

It is Shabbat
the still point
at the turn of an in-breath.

How the losses mount up
your mother, father
now Denise and Chloe too.

Don't fight
the pull toward
nothingness.

It's the light
from your own hand
that stops your fall

flickering
burning up the wick
and flaring.

Sabbath Bride

My wife is late getting home from her clinic
my son makes fake gurgling sounds
all through the *brucha* as I try on
my ludicrous paterfamilias imitation.

But the crisp imperfect piece of red pepper
I nervously pick from the salad
changes from bitter to sweet on my tongue.
The just-blessed wine goes to work

on the tense muscles in my neck
and the newly-kindled candles
shine on the soft place I love
just below your cheekbone.

Shabbes Eve

The moon is rummaging around the garden
Splintering the bean poles, knocking the old gate
Off its hinges, drinking the beer I left out
For the slugs. It's the flat of tomato starts

She's after, so I threw a sheet over them
At bedtime. They say the blood orange moon will
Drink the piss out of your body, but don't think

The jilted bride moon is much better, snagging
her veil on the bougainvillea then flailing
At the window, jittering the points that hold

The panes in place. Don't be angry, Shekinah.
I'm a wayward husband, drunk half the week, but
I left you some challah out on the table.

The Tell

Psychologists and cops
CIA types, guys who won
the World Series of Poker
cranks with a theory
the blind guy with
his Braille Tarot
analysts with
proprietary algorithms
hunched over scholars
of the Talmud
teleological experts
Cray Computer armed
statisticians, none
can beat a coin flip
when it comes to knowing
the mind of God.
Has He decided?
Is He fair? Is He really
there at all? You reach
through the vineyard fence
to steal a single grape—
Which? Perplexed
but the hand knows
this one's perfect
so cool
with just the right hint
of sugar.

Six Quatrains

Brilliant Silence

A high mountain meadow still brown from the winter
Dead heading log truck back from the mill
Then a silence so deep it dares you to enter
And bind your small self to His will

Faith

Press the eyeballs: chaos
End the pressure form returns
Press the heart and God betrays us
But only till the dross is burned

Funhouse Mirror

We call for security and security comes
But they frisk the wrong man and break both his thumbs
We call for a deity and a deity comes
Who just asks for forgiveness and begs for our crumbs.

Prayer of Intercession

God save us from the willful destruction of others
And the destruction we wreak on ourselves
And the destruction we merely uncover
While digging our personal hells.

Visitors

Someone knocks at 3 a.m. "Who's there?"
But my thick gums are word dams.
What if it's God's son, answering my prayer?
But they go for Bobbie, Jake grabs them, I duct tape their hands.

Train Whistle

That train that wakes you—take it
You'll be in the Yuba City yard by dawn
Snow geese in the derelict feedlot
A sheetmetal warehouse catching the sun.

Walk

I walk along Alhambra past the Safeway
And CVS, on past the strip mall card club
And the asphalt junior high that looks to me
Like a repurposed army base. Everywhere God

The Bal Shem taught, sunlight on the parking lot
The fat geese by the fountain, the ivy walled
Branch library, every word in every book
The bound Delta hydrology reports, Leaves

Of Grass the deathbed edition, bound Sunsets
From the fifties in their yearly cardboard sleeves.
A cool drink from the old porcelain fountain

And I'm on my way, past the park, a broad leaf
Maple, trikes on lawn, new waxed Silverado
Curtains billowing, someone's music playing.

Asymptote

Little chickens jump on spoons
to play a wineglass xylophone.
I'd been reading a book on hermeneutics
when Cartoon Network mysteriously clicked on.
Puffy mice join in the raucous chorus.
Is language, Gadamer asks, a bridge or a barrier?
A bridge he maintains, through which
we can know ourselves in the being of the other.
When her husband left her my neighbor
spent days sorting bolts and screws:
number four hex heads, half round number sixes.
It seems to me we're approaching God
as an asymptote. Our calculations are getting
ever more precise, but we are running out of time.
Eventually she moved to Oregon, just kept driving
until she found a place she liked, in, no kidding,
Sweet Home. *The fusion of horizons* is G's telling
phrase for the nature of understanding.
The kitchen fills up with chicks
and mice for the madcap crescendo:
they pop out of drawers, poke
through the flute of the teakettle.

At the Dog Park

The ridgeback was trying
to hump the labradoodle
while the little sheltie
was yapping at their paws
trying to herd them.
I wanted to herd my little
family too, but the boys
never call and my wife's
in Arizona. The Lord is my
sheltie, I laughed to myself
as an orange blazon
ranged around the Bay
from Mount Tam
to the San Mateo Bridge.
I felt calm then
my lust and shame
fell into line and heeled.
As it says in the Zohar
All the tangles combed smooth.

III

A GREAT BLUE HERON
IN BOYNTON BEACH

Spared

There's no telling how
many things I've been spared.
A brain-stem stroke
humiliating interrogations
by the police in a country
where I'd come to do research.
I have not been predeceased
by my children
I had no money in Ponzi schemes
There are no viral videos circulating
of me in compromising situations.
I am not catheterized, cuckolded
my ten–year-in-the-making autobiographical novel
has not just been remaindered.
I am not currently undergoing
a dark night of the soul
I am no more worried than the next guy
by global warming, the resurgence of French anti-Semitism
or the miasmic air in Shandong Province China.
Although I met someone I couldn't place today
who talked animatedly about how glad
he was to see me, I've so far been spared
the worst ravages of memory loss.
I guess a six I told the triage nurse at Kaiser
about the pain in my twisted ankle
sparing me the I.V. concoction
they reserve for seven or higher.
I've been spared finding out
if the green flash at sunset is the same light
as you see when you're dying
and I've been spared hovering
over my own funeral listening

to a eulogy that contains factual errors.
But can we be spared from having to be spared?
I've read a lot of unconvincing books
but maybe yes I thought once
watching this Thai monk at Spirit Rock
laugh from the heart of his belly.

To My Posthumous Readers

I'm interested in who you are
and how you found me.
Was it my cousin's kids
who kept my name alive?
Did you find an interesting
clip online, maybe even a
still-existing bookstore
where Shaddock and Shelley
could touch covers
and share a markdown?
I used to write poems on nights like this
clear, early fall, during the last quarter
or, hopefully, third of my life
when I suffered from mid-sleep-cycle
insomnia. I would imagine
a great lyric: the fixed stars
looking down, not with
disdain, but charity.
Why else would we evolve
the capacity to sense the uncanny
if not to record occasions like this
when we feel lifted up
loved beyond our merit
freed from the tyranny of if/then
the Cyrillic alphabet stars
suddenly comprehensible
like the time on acid I saw
Yevtushenko in Pauley Ballroom
and thought I understood every word?

Heretics

The heliophobic part of me that agrees
with the Cathars that this world
itself is the problem balked this morning
when I tried to take it out for breakfast
to this fishermen's café I know
where they serve mounds of hash browns
half the size of Everest and refill your coffee
the minute it's an inch below the rim.
If we're all just hogs with tags in our ears here
why rush to the feedlot?
Even as a kid I knew enough
to quit my job on the consciousness farm
and stick instead to Saint Fuck-This-Shit.
I've managed through the years
not to succumb and take the pills
that would kill my refusal.
Now there are others like me
not just Raskolnikov knockoffs
but shipping clerks and bike messengers
even a few doctors and clergy.
We believe the glow in our grudge
is Christ the redeemer of foundries and feedlots.

Executive Decision

So a Civic cuts off a Crown Vic
near Hilltop Mall
and the guy in the Ford
follows him off the ramp
squeezes off a few rounds
and kills his eight-year-old son.
This happened on Tuesday.
My desk was already cluttered
with items like this
the G.I. who went postal in Kandahar
the weekly list of crappy acts I get from Amnesty
when something snapped for Me
and I decided to revoke Free Will for man.
All they'll feel at first is a strange lethargy
as every day becomes exactly like the last
but soon enough they'll notice their fists won't ball up
their tongues grow fat as mackerel when they try and curse Me.
They'll never change jobs again
and too bad for the next Mozart, he's written his last note.
They're wasting their time praying now.
I've looped some Gregorian chants on my voicemail
and put the hotline on permanent busy.

"A Kind of Divine Psychoanalysis"

I heard that Reb Nachman of Breslav, who apparently suffered from depression, used to go out to a field a long way from his village and let God have it. I decided to try it myself. It took a while to get rolling, but after a bit I really started to let it fly. I asked God why he blessed the shits and cursed me. I told him my vision of a conga line of assholes, waving their thumb over their finger in the gimme the dough gesture, and God obligingly passing out the green. I wondered out loud if He got a kick out of kicking me. I even started to blaspheme, hurling fbomb after fbomb heavenward. After a while I began to shake and cry inconsolably. You did this to me, you bastard, it's your fault I'm so fucked up. I felt like a seventeen-year-old coming down on a couple of Bennies. As I hooked up my dog to continue my walk toward a morning latte, the corniest thing happened—the rocks seemed to quiver with aliveness, the birdsong rivaled anything I'd heard from Bach. What's next, I wondered, are God and I going to have make-up sex? But no need to make up, everything was fine already. I even forgave the tuneless banjo gal outside Peets, whose grating rendition of "May the Circle Be Unbroken" spoke to me like she was Hendrix or something.

It Hits You

1.

You're sorting out a color load
in the laundry room for instance
when it hits you
that humans are probably
an evolutionary mistake
in the process of being
corrected. But Ben
you go remembering
with a pleasure tingle
taking your eight year old
grandson to the A's game
last weekend. Quiet in the car
all the way back to Sacramento
raveling and unraveling
the world in his mind.

2.

Snow geese, salmon, caribou, puffin
harp seal, narwhal, possum
pika, Apollo butterfly, incense
cedar, sea turtles, all frogs
newts and salamanders. The mirror
neuron system, which repeats
in our own brains
the neural pathways of other's
movement, is thought
by some to be the source
of our moral imagination. A rising
of migratory birds from the rice fields

so vast the wings create wind
and in the squall of their voices
you can barely hear yourself talk.

3.

I know someone who says
it would be better for humans to die out
and save the animals from extinction.
Hey Grandpa, says Ben
breaking the silence. When
Cespedes was yelling
in Spanish after he struck out
do you think the umpire
could understand him?

January Storm

Hail on the deck, the Monterey pines
in a wind-driven frenzy.
An hour later, bright sunshine
glowing cumulous, mist rising
like smoke from the redwood deckboards.
The rhythm of these January storms
shows up in my college notebooks:
Storm after storm from the northwest,
sunlight and torrential rain.
My p-coat soaked, light prismed
by the rain on my glasses.
Reached the fire trail as the acid was coming on
sunset beneath dark clouds, a big storm approaching.
Not much older than my son is now
with his makeup and made up Facebook homepage.
The storms will drop over Tamalpais, darkening the Bay
when he's in his twenties, gone mad for women
in his thirties, when he's laid off and
and blames me for everything.
They'll slam my grave, than his as well
the Pacific High drifting northward
warm air from South Asia hitting
an anticyclone front from Alaska
water spouts near Hawaii, fifty foot swells
homing in, the southern sky darkening
the windows of the hillside houses
beginning to rattle.

For the Dyings

There are so many little dyings, it doesn't matter which of them is death
—Kenneth Rextroth

For the dyings
        are grace
                formed by our moving

out of peril
        into vanquished
                certainty

a space
        between the piano notes
                when the yearning

in your eyes
        meets
                the yearning

in mine
        and we are slain.
                It is a way

out
        so different
                from the annihilations

we worked
        on each other
                through lovemaking

yet it is certainly
        the death
                of everything

we have been.
      Waking—
            new lines

in your face
      hold me to
            you like wire.

Woman I love
      there is no mourning
            our deaths

this morning
      the rain
            breaks on the textured

hills
      a moment
            revealing
their flesh
      still
            manifest

as ours is.
      Tremors
            our hearts

stop
      at every
            beat.

Tree of Life

What a relief to think the body itself
Is an allegory, a glyph of journey
From fact to form, and then, if God is willing
Back again. Knees and feet are transit hubs, groin

A great gathering hall, hips the ruins of two
Quite different cities, one known for its art
And hope, the other for its massive projects
Of civic good. They feed a spot above our

Diaphragm, where beauty cradles the heart
That pumps out love and then returns with judgement.
Your right arm plants, your left arm harvests

The poem lifts off from the top of your head.
So much better than dank breath and achy limbs
After three flu-filled nights and days, lying in bed.

After Psalm 50: *For the World Is Mine, and the Fulness Thereof*

We keep going round and round, YaH. I say give
Me a sign, you say give me thanks and praise. It's
Almost like a bad marriage. I'd love you more
If only. And then these late fall sunsets break

My heart, dazzling fans of ochre spread out
From the Gate, rolling to peach and pale yellow
At the tip of the cloudbank. Now *The heavens
Declare your righteousness*. You say don't give me

Your little gifts, your halfhearted offerings
Of faith, for every ounce of this fulness
Is already my tribute. I think You are

Asking what love everywhere entails: just look
At the world through my eyes, give thanks when you
Hear the red tail hawk scree at dawn for his mate.

Plan

Everyone tells you to live in the present
But I want there to be a plan, not a mere
Stream of nameless sensation. I want running
Sap through the bast, the thirsty taproot sucking

Groundwater, the roundworms shitting soil, the vast
Mycelial networks linking tree to tree
Not just the new orange feathery catkins
Shedding pollen like rain on a late spring day

In Northern California. I want it
All to be part of a plan, unfolding in
A mind vaster than a billion networked Cray

Computers, foreseen, tucked into some
Inclusive consciousness that defines, by its
Presence, love, that pours down and makes me shudder.

Morning Blessings

The panting dog's tongue by my bedside
invites a blessing for the imminent dawn
so I offer a *bracha* for the brain stem
that battled entropy all night
on my behalf and for the waking
that vanished the endless recession
of cellblocks I was walking.
Blessings upon my nether, pleasure parts
that double as effluent outlets
and for the ordinance that bans
trash pickup before seven.
I bless the medicines
that soothe or jumpstart
my various organs, that find
my son at sea and return him
safely to port, and I bless
the tickle of air across cilia
the circulation of blood
in my blessedly still-open arteries.
My message-free cellphone blesses me
with no news of death or airplane calamity.
Blessings on my books, the window,
the furnace kicking on
the strew of happily used clothing
in my hamper. And a blessing
for consciousness itself
this string of recursive synapses
that discards the neural dross
and brings me the world, just as it is.

After Psalm 23

Even on a sunny day death's shadow looms.
A car careens, a mugger lurks, something turns
Up on a routine lab test. Yet here I am
Across the street, ready to lead my old dog

For a run in the park, ready for a cool
Drink from the fountain. Why not believe it's your
Strength I lean on, that fear of your rebuke stays
My greed and malice? Even the dark valleys

I create for myself so far have always
Brightened, and the sharp pains of my losses have dulled
Just as your consoling voice in my mind's ear

Promised. Will my kids have jobs or stay off drugs?
Will my love and I have a few more unvexed
Years? It's your voice I hear saying yes, we will.

A Great Blue Heron in Boynton Beach

Camrys in the lantana shade
pock of yellow balls on green courts
splash of water aerobics
talk of total knees and hips replaced
the blind psychiatrist working his way
past the gauntlet of kibitzers to his favorite chaise:
all this is pleasing to the higher orders
who would themselves like soon to retire.
Tif'eret, compassion, Binah, the womb of the world,
are worn out at the end of a bloody century.
A great blue heron's six-foot wings
cast a shadow over the pool
granting a moment's respite from the sun
for the second generation furriers and insurance men
whose five-year-old granddaughters in pink-frilled two-pieces
swim like a fish, their red-polished nails breaking the surface.
A *machaia,* really, to be ever so briefly in shade
to stop thinking about all that is lost
and believe, along with the Kaballists
that the Eternal One's thirst is slaked by our pleasure.

IV

IN THIS PLACE WHERE
SOMETHING'S MISSING LIVES

In This Place Where *Something's Missing* Lives

This question of where I am in my world is outwardly one that a person can ask himself, but inwardly it is the voice of God speaking to man: to man who has lost his way. ...This ...is the response to despair, to the unanswered plea of the bereaved and bewildered, to the lost son who cannot find a home. It is the Other Voice asking the very same question.

Adin Steinsaltz,
The Thirteen Petalled Rose

1.

I live companioned with longing.
He sits when I sit, stands
when I go to the door
to look after some imagined sound.

What is your name?
I ask my companion again,
and tonight, instead of *absence*
he answers *rapture*.

Could this be the moment—
of exile's
apogee?

2.

I envision a light source
spiraling from a single point
out through all the galaxies of the Universe,

but always it is stopped
by the opaque wall
of my skin.

In inner darkness, desire,

molecular, unthreads,
reaches for some unknown nutrient.

What do You want of me
with Your talk of the Holy Sparks
in each particular thought?

Why do You keep after me
asking this emptiness
to procreate?

Is it that You are born
in the place where
I deny You,

that this "husk",
this fear in my belly
that I have tried so long to discard,

is the place where these
Sparks gather and ready
their leap into existence?

3.

> *This is like the person who is counting money while his children are being*
> *held for ransom. They come to him and say, "You have money! Ransom us!"*
> —The Baal Shem Tov

It is true, as You accuse me.
My children are crying, and I
am hoarding little portions
of this universe, saying this

is mine, don't take it.

I feel them, the innocent ones,
the unborn. I don't know
what they want from me.
I can go back and mark out
in black ink every thought
that does not serve their well-being.

But I have erased this page
and all my pages.
I know their eyes, pleading
for me to lose my mind
and love them, to believe them
into existence.

But I do not believe.
I sit in my counting house,
where the children's cries are a dim echo,
searching for the cause of deficits.

4.

> When a person has pain, whether physical or spiritual, he should meditate
> that even in this pain, God can be found. He is only concealed in a garment
> in this pain. When a person realizes this, then he can remove the garment.
> —The Baal Shem Tov

When I do not run from grief
I am kin to all that bleeds
its beauty into the world: salmon
smashing their silver bodies against the sluice gate,
the tree of dying Monarchs I saw in Big Sur,

the bearded, glaze-eyed everyman
standing palm out in the rail-station doorway.

I do not want to find You
in some 'Supernal Mansion',
but here on the earth,
where every living being
is clothed in the raiment of its death.
I do not want to 'shed the garment'
but to wear my grief like skin,
alive and permeable.

5.

> *He is only concealed in a garment in this Pain.*
> Toby Shaddock, 1913-1986

I remember your living touch on my hand.
I see you as I saw you the last time,
in the hospital, wires cut
into every part of your body.

I am no less afraid of your dying
than I was before your death,
for each reliving is as fearful
as your passing.

Yet when I let myself
be with your absence
I begin to feel consoled.

A word, a syllable
presses on my lips

as if seeking release.

Could Your name now
be a passage
out of grief's labyrinth?

6.

Thou shalt call understanding mother.
based on Proverbs 2:3

Thin arms of purple fuchsia
grow up through the spruce-hedge,
bending and swaying in the heavy fog.

Mile Rock Horn, Alcatraz,
the Gate Bridge pylons,
sound one after another,

the silence of the interstices
cold as the space
behind my heart.

I want to call you.
I reach for the phone,
half-forgetting you are two-years dead.

I am always reaching out
and falling back
into this cold center of gravity.

I want you to tell me
that this reaching and falling
is exactly the measure I was born to.

I want to feel cold fog on my skin,
to accept its breath
as the flower does,

swaying in the certainty
of nurture
and destruction.

7.

The white phosphorous bombs.
The bone-seeking fire.
The rubber bullets and swinging batons,
the trainwheels cutting a man's legs.

I do not accuse You.
I live uneasily with my despair.

Yet some days I am still moved to hope,
against the news of perpetual pogrom,
that something other than this fist
in men's hearts will prevail.

Elohim, God of mercy,
is it in hoping that You exist
that You exist,
this longing itself
Your in-dwelling spark?

8.

I would come back to this place
where *something's missing* lives
and feel the cold fog
touch the hollow of my bones,
and listen in the interstices
between heartbeats
for the cry of an inconsolable infant
and know again why I must invent my God.

I remember the time I first knew this,
almost twenty years ago,
on the commuter bus in Brighton,
smelling the wet wool of all the coats,
pressed up against the inviolable boundary
of so many solitudes,
and feeling the infinity of my own.

I did not know then
that I would not find You
in prayer, or vision, or even
as consolation to my great sorrow.
I did not know then that this yearning
was visitation,
that the exhaustion of all my hope
of finding something Holy
was nothing but a step
toward pride's renunciation.

Today, as I look at
the vibram-sole prints
I leave in slushy snow,
or feel the icy water penetrate

my thick wool socks,
and find again the surety that
I will walk on with no destination
but a moment's respite at a dairy bar
for a hot cup of borscht,
I feel myself alive again
in the body of Your absence.

I am ready now to cry out to You
in a voice that is not my own,
in a voice that carves a hollow in my chest,
a dwelling, a hearth
that waits an eon
or an instant
for Your kindling breath.

9.

Wisdom comes into being from Nothing.
　　　　　　　　　　　—Job 28:12

The silence that follows a day of steady rain
is a kind of questioning.

It seeps into me like fog,
erasing all the world.

It is delicious to surrender to it,
Ain Soph, Nothing of Nothings, at my back

while at my front I await
the arrival of a kiss.

10.

It is broken. Don't
even try to fix it.

What we'd dreamed of,
perfect love, lies

on the workbench
like a hopeless pile of watchworks.

This smashed case, this
diaspora of gears and springs

are the very sparks
of the Holy.

God wanted it thus, each
of us uniquely broken,

uniquely most His
in our moment of greatest exile.

11.

In the space between the pink plum blossoms
and the thick leaves of the loquat tree,
a gray February sky is burst by beams of gold light.

I want to leave off this dialogue
with a God I can't be sure exists
and go into that light.

But I cannot. Inside my chest
is a fist, clenching darkness,
that has been brandished for a thousand years.

Towhees dive past the window.
Their God is not the God of the Jews.
No Hasid, laughing and dancing,

is as oblivious as a bird.
And no bird shoulders the world's sorrow
like a Zaddik, lifting the bride's chair at a wedding.

I want to lay down my burden.
But even joy remembers and burns
like a Yahrtzeit candle in my chest.

12.

> *Know that when you pray in the fields, all the grasses come into your*
> *prayers. They help you and give you strength to pray.*
> —Rabbi Nachman

On the porch, across the scrubby meadow,
the innkeeper's daughters improvise a dance,
their red skirts twirling in the morning sunlight.

I remember my own childhood
and begin to sink into familiar grief.
But something in the air arrests me—

the spicy bay smell of the North Coast woods—
and brings back a time before I was broken,
when I lived alone on Sea View Road

reading Dante and cutting firewood. I remember
the orchard ground covered with yellow mustard,
the long exaltation of the blooming sourgrass.

I feel that memory, alive, like a seed in the earth,
beneath the detritus of accumulated loss.
These whacked down, resurgent trees,

the meadow grasses half turning in the breeze,
even the ear-shaped fungi growing on the deadfalls
come into me now, strengthen my prayer,

which is simply to stay here,
to be open to all that utters the blessing: *I live*
just one moment longer.

13.

I meditate every night on my bed in tears
                              —Psalms 6:7

How can I beg You not to go,
to stay here and comfort me,
when we haven't finished our argument?

I feel like a foolish husband
caught bluffing, panicking that this time
his wife will take him seriously.

What were the terms of our argument?
I wanted a sign, some knowledge
that You exist separate from my needing You.
You wanted prayer, a miming of belief.

Tonight, twisting in the bed-linen
like an auger, boring a hole
in the fabric of this world,
I have lost the will to fight.

I do not know what it means
to be 'born again', but I want
to *be* born, to struggle
to the end of this tunnel,

to find someone waiting there,
some living source of kindness
that just fits this shape of need my mouth makes.

14.

When we remember the magnificence of the divine revelation in the days
when the temple was standing and all the beauty and glory we enjoyed at
that time, the soul inside us weeps and our hearts feel deep sorrow... and
through this process we are purified.

—Rabbi Levi of Berditchev

We broke the glass at our wedding
to remember then that even this
our greatest joy was a shard
of the broken City.

Now when months of barrenness
have us at each other's throats,
we remember that this grief
is a fragment also,

an atom of the loss we all
have suffered in our exile
from the Holy City.
Ah God, I wanted happiness.
Instead I've found sorrow.
Are You there, waiting,
wondering when I'll realize

that what I've yearned for
all my life is near at hand,
is as free as Your blessing,
as free as running water, as moving air.

15.

> *The Shekinah ... wishes to dwell below.*
> —Adin Steinsaltz

First light, a waning moon
on the western horizon,
white against pale blue.

My hand under your shoulder,
I feel your breath through my arm
pulling my breath into synchrony.

Now love comes without effort,
amber light drawn down
through your body into mine.

How grateful I feel, after a season
of harshness, when our love
becomes again the vessel.

16.

Prayer is a sexual coupling with the Shekinah
—attributed to The Baal Shem Tov

Palm fit to curves,
each sinew anew,
tickle of stubble,

knee, thigh,
the tip
of your hip.

Once again
you are
You,

Emanation,
to teach me again
the holy of joy,

the sin of
depression
I hide within.

17.

Is this also
        a prayer,
                the cry

of the shipwrecked,
        of the ones who journey

                    forever and never

find the bride?
          Is it their song
                    that lingers in the air

like the echoing
          chant of the cantor
                    in the Shul rafters?

18.

i.

Jan Pearce singing Kol Nidre on the Ed Sullivan Show—
Aunt Betty not knitting
Daddy awake in his armchair
Mother stopping her ironing
all the turmoil in the house
stilled for a moment by ancient song
emanating from the wraithlike image
on the twelve inch black and white.

ii.

In the bottom of my desk's detritus, beside
dried pens, used stamps and paper clips,
wrapped in cellophane and sealed with a rubber-band:
eighteen cents—

my mother's charm for travelers,
eighteen kopek'd sons returned safe from the Tzar's army,

Moishe and Dave safe on the trip from Poltava to Winnipeg,
Luba and the children following in steerage,
all eighteen-cented and safe—

thrown down distractedly by me years ago
after some coastal hitch-hike,
now bidding me fare forward
from beyond her grave.

iii.

Eighteen the sum of the letters *chet* and *yod,*
thus, in the thinking of Kabbalah,
the number for *chayim,* for life.

I think of my mother, clutching her jade,
her gold *chai* charm, her eyes
holding me with fear,
O, David, am I going to die?

iv.

It is late on the eve of this new year.
I feel my Jewishness live in me
as a cry of sorrow rising from the old house's
tangled history. I am afraid of life,
afraid of the holocaust that lurks
at the edge of every heartbeat.

I hold the cellophane-wrapped coins in my hand,
feeling their weight and temperature.
My heart is peeled back, layer upon layer of grief,

to find this minute, still-vivid, in-dwelling.
Therefore have I set life and death before you
that you may choose life.

Deut. 29:19

19.

When will I be worthy for the light of the
Divine Presence to dwell with me?
—The Baal Shem Tov

Hot October. The sun's rays
parallel to the horizon
burn into my forehead.

So much to erase,
the constant hiding,
the shams I pile on shame.

What's left
but this yearning
to be worthy of love?

Will you be with me,
here where we wait
at the start of a year

for the doors to open,
for wind and a drop
of cooling wine?

20.

He who speaks falsehood shall not be established before my eyes.
—Psalms 101:7

We live in the capital of malice
and watch the tall buildings
greedily suck light
from the hearts of the populace.

The Lieutenant Colonel
jabs the air, conducting
an orchestra of falsehoods.
Are You hidden in his lips,

in the machete hand
of the Contra assassin?
Are You hidden in the part of me
that is itself a lie,

that asserts coherence
and mastery of a world
that shatters and is remade
with every breath?

This is a city of lies
and I am its citizen.
I walk the streets, ruse
meeting the eyes of ruse.

Are You near me now
when I know there is no witness
when I have no plan for assembling
the shards I have called my self?

21.

All the world is just a narrow bridge
—Rabbi Nachman

An old Geographic photo
of a Tibetan rope bridge,
a family crossing,

possessions on their heads,
feet on a two-inch cord
above a thousand meter chasm.

There is in their step,
though they spend their days wandering,
no hint of the gait of exile,

while for me every footfall
is minced by the fear
of falling off the world.

Weary with another
year's passing,
I think of surrendering

to gravity, giving
myself up to fall
into the center of my losses.

Would I spiral forever?
Or find, in the midst
of free-fall, how

to spread arms and soar,
as if prayer were a wing I'd carried in my body from birth.

High Holy Days, 5748

22.

There is a language in which
You speak of Your need for me,
half understood, the gist caught like lip-reading.
It comes at the boundary of my senses,
a brush of wind across my neck,
a thrill that lingers in my chest between heartbeats,
the echo of sorrow, sounding in the well of my abdomen,
telling me that there is a bottom,
that there is water there.

Sometimes the syntax is incomprehensible,
the flashes of gleaned meaning evaporate like dreams.
Other times I do not want to comprehend
the sentence that unnames my world,
that leaves me alone here in the first light,
wondering at every sound,
waiting for one of them to be Your voice
calling in the wind
David, where are you?

V

SPLENDOR

SPLENDOR

1. *Come and See*

The potato vine blossoms grow white on the fence rail.
The redwood boughs flex and return on the wind.
The early spring rain girds the eaves in pearls.
To the *beings up above and the creatures down below*
Zohar 1:103

I say Hello! Hello!
This is the living Torah that unspools from a point
in my chest, two fingers below the heart.
What's to become of me?
Take wing, take wing
I've grown old with no wisdom
Take wing, take wing
Flashing, disappearing   Ezekial, 1:14
The radiance zaps you in the wilderness
finds you there, worshipping your losses
Take wing, Take wing
The beings the prophet saw had four faces
corresponding to the four levels of existence:
Matter, Soul, Spirit and Essence
among which they moved as messengers
declaring, however faintly, a human possibility
glimpsed forty years ago in Muir Woods reverie
the old growth redwoods breathing
the sky a phantasmagoria of color
and a point, fascinating, not terrifying
beyond which all things simply ceased.
Come and see:
Even now, in the midst of staid life
the radiance zaps me as the dusk sky brightens
behind the swaying oak tree.

2. Dream + Interpretation

i.

In my dream my son and I
are lost in a city. We climb down
the crumbling brickwork of a parking structure
toward a street with run down streetcar lines
and an old dollar store.
He seems (as is true in life) less perturbed than me
but not exactly unperturbed.

ii.

Brokenness, in the Kabbalah of Isaac Luria
refers to the vessels that could not hold
the primal light. So the tracks blown with litter
the crumbling brickwork, the downtrodden
discount store are holy, sacred in their loneliness.
But it's his hand in mine
facing the blasted landscape
going somehow forward
that remains the center of the dream.

3. On the Train

Then it was called Elohim, hidden and concealed
Zohar 1:29

All of us with our jaws gone slack as the train
lulls us to sleep, all of us on our cell phones
typing GTG now, all of us pretending

86

to exist as monads or accidents
skulls under hair or hoods or stocking caps
crammed to the jimmies with every which
kind of longing, including this one
that wants simply to rise, even as the Beloved
longs to descend.
She's the one with the elegant coat and the leather backpack.
She's the curl of a lip
silently miming a headphoned song.
She's the flash of sunlight off the girders just before
the train goes into a tunnel.
This is what Jacob saw, what we live now
the angelic messengers rising and falling
the flash of recognition as spirit descends
and the arduous, human ascent, as in Denise's poem:
and a man climbing
must scrape his knees, and bring
his hands into play.

4. The Wedding

> *She enters, escorted by her maidens*
> Zohar 1:8a

A scrub jay squabbles in the alder.
The ubiquitous sound of city jackhammers.
The old oak's pattern of light
and shadow across the field.
The kaballists say *lift up this world*
like the bride at a wedding
her long hair flying
as the chair rises and falls.
Now the groomsmen grab me up as well—

87

stop holding the chair for dear life they shout—
and soon I'm waving my kippa like a sombrero.
Holding on to a white handkerchief
we spiral around each other on the saxophone horah
of the r & b band.
Now that she has entered the canopy,
she is called glory   Zohar 1:8a
A slight breeze ripples the shadows of the oak leaves.
All these years later
sitting in a park in Berkeley
remembered ecstasy calling me to prayer
like the muezzin from a distant minaret.

5. In Tilden

> *The light that shines when the King visits the doe*
> Zohar 1:4a

Twin fawns, almost yearlings
leap from the eucalyptus
Twenty feet from the guardrail
freckled ears alert
heads turned in perfect symmetry
steady black eyes holding mine.
The rising sun backlights the ridgetop.
O low, sleeping ones, closed eyed, awake   Zohar 1:4a
the old text implores us
as if consciousness itself
turns darkness into light
bitter into sweet.

6. Eyes

It is the light of the eye
Zohar 1:31:b

The light rises over the forested hilltops
and shines on the grid of apartments
and soldier stanchions of the Richmond Bridge.
It backlights the refinery smokestacks
and silvers the calm estuary.
It is the first light, the old eye
but also—here the text is most explicit—
your eyes, rheumy, myopic
viewing their creation.

7. *Come and See:*

The dark Bay like a rest in a tone poem.
Then the crescendo of lights, the baseball stadium,
The brightlit highrises, the cruciform
Radio tower. And beyond these,
On this clear night in early spring:
These are the heavens and their array   Zohar 1:1b
the work of the Blessed Holy One.

8. On "The Other Side"

They tortured his legs with shackles,
His neck was put in iron.
Psalm 105, tr. Robert Alter

The men who break the prisoner's spirit
themselves are broken. They will not
be returned to the ranks of men.
They who drown and sodomize
have gone too far to the Other Side
to find their way back.
They are split off, pure reason
divorced from imagination, as Blake saw
unable to imagine the fruit
of their ill labor, the breaking
of a man's soul, and themselves
broken, loosed upon the world.

9. The Demon

Compassion has vanished, transformed into judgment
Zohar I:120a (commentary on the binding of Isaac)

Children in cages, dragged screaming from their parents.
You don't need the sound on to understand him
the sneer, the glee at the powerless
squirming before him, Fox and Friends flickering
as he finishes his morning coffee.
There is a progress to our diminution
from shame to outrage to a thirst
that only power, and not even that
will quench. Every morning
I pass the old woman sweeping up
the sycamore leaves outside the preschool
the laughing truckers delivering potted trees
to Northbrae nursery and think how
they must flinch these days
when an unmarked white car goes by.

Is this demon a part of ourselves
unloved, unlovable, incapable of loving?
How could it not be
when God himself tells
a father to cut his own son's throat ?

10. Confirmation Hearing

It is this yearning from below which brings about the completion above.
Zohar, tr. Gershom Sholem

Between the victim's "was that answer helpful"
and the accused judge's flaring nostrils
it is hard to remember that God
is nothing
but the balance in our hearts
between *Din* (judgment)
And *Hesid* (lovingkindness).
"I remember their laughter afterward
as they drunkenly bounced
against the stairwell."

What does the tree of knowledge
of good and evil mean?   Zohar 1:135a
the Zohar asks.
Sweet and bitter ...
it suckles on two sides.

As if there were a spark
inside our revulsion
from which beauty flows
into the world "as from a single river"

91

where love's chaos is bounded
and two lovers vow
to cherish and protect
one another.

11. Albany Bulb

An industrial marsh at low tide—
half rounds of truck tires
old railroad ties
Styrofoam net floats
chunks of concrete
trailing Giacometti writhings of rebar.
Headlights from the guardrail reflectors
catch an egret's white wings
as he rises.
This shame, seemingly inescapable
for what we've done to the world—
merely a husk.

12. A Visit

At anchor, Nimbus spins first to the wind
then to the current. I spend the night
loading bricks onto a wheelbarrow.
Some have gobs of mortar still attached.
An old guy in some kind of loin cloth
apparently the overseer
sensing my confusion, tells me to remember
the world is nothing but love
and consciousness, by which I understand
him to mean the endless iteration
of need and form. I wake

feeling strangely comforted
the wind pinning the fog against the hills
cormorants and gulls in the tide rip
The boat straining the rode up into the breeze
then slowly drifting down again.

13. Mercy

*Even the tiniest thing in this world depends on another, supernal thing
appointed over it*
                                                    Zohar, I: 156b

A pharmacy receipt for Diet Coke and Kleenex
an Arizona commemorative quarter
the Universal Declaration on the Rights of Men
the light-refracting shards of a broken Mickey's Big Mouth

*Nothing in this world alone, untwinned
nothing in the other unmoved
by our existence*

birdshit on a Prius
your headache transmitting neurons
the talc-like sands of Afghanistan
discarded petroleum barrels on the Siberian steppes

All involved in a cosmic pas de deux

a free hydroxyl radical in the bloodstream
a prom photo with the boy carefully cut out
a bit of gristle caught in your teeth

Not some indifferent digital

registration above
click for click
but God's mercy, overflowing

burnt trash
fig tree
the Ring Nebula in Orion.

14. By the River of Already

> *I was in the midst of exile…by the River of Already*
> Zohar, 1:6b

i.

By the River of Already, we sit
and count our sleights and losses
you let the tea steep too long
now it's too bitter to drink
you forget to buy forever stamps
on the last day they're sold
those swollen glands could mean cancer
this isn't at all what I'm after
the editor scrawls on your manuscript.

By the River of Already
the dead hold legendary parties,
each with a theme—Samba
your favorite movie stars—
but by the time you remember them
the date has come and gone.

ii.

It could be any river, even the gold-flecked American
at sundown, willow and cottonwood
reflected in the slow ripples.
it doesn't take the guy ripping through
on a Skidoo with the muffler off
or the sounds of the distant sand quarry
which you notice and now can't get out of your head
to remind you of all that is lost.
You sit on a plastic beach chair
trying to make sense, always trying
to make sense, though it is not
a reckoning, or even reconciliation
you are after, but a sense
of possibility, that *the time of singing has arrived*
                                    Song of Songs 2:12

as when grandpa showed up
with bagels and chopped liver
to the house on Chautauqua
on Sunday morning
so delicious everyone stopped fighting
while they were eating.

iii.

By the River of Already,
time flows only in one direction.
Though you see the form
the poem could take
and feel the excitement
run from your brain
to your arm to your fingertips

it is gone by the time
you are set to start writing.

iv.

You've heard the rumors of the other river
the River of Now, which flows
in mythic time and bestows
Sheffa, its blessings on the world.
In truth it's the same river.
You put your fingers to your lips
hushing loss as if it were a noisy visitor
who forgot the baby was asleep.
"She is not afraid"   Proverbs 31:21
and in her presence we are not either—
the poem we thought lost
found in a drawer
on a forgotten flash drive
the words buoyed up, carried on
toward a point just beyond
anticipation.
This is the one world we have
fed by a single river
the variegated beach gravel
a breeze in the reeds
in the crowns of the cottonwoods.

15. Word

"The word flies, ascending and descending, and it is transformed into a heaven."

Zohar, 1:5a

Come and see
how every thing that exists
carries buried within the longing to return.
This is the truth under the words, that
they long to fly free from their tether.
The stoic rocks bear up, the animals in the great
wheel of their existence barely feel it
but we, at our peril, grab on, grab on
trying to deny the lightness within.
Come and see that even as matter encloses us
the Blessed Holy One in his love and loneliness
longs to descend, waits eagerly all week
for his invitation.
Take wing, Take wing
The blossoms have appeared on earth   Song of Songs 2:12
The voice of the turtledove is heard in our land.
Come and see:
This voice is heard, *a voice sculpting a spoken word*
Rendering her perfect.   Zohar 1:98a
Not the hazan, but my own voice
greeting
the January clouds
backlit at sundown
dark bars of rain descending
out past the Gate.

Notes

p. 23. North Fork of the Tuolumne River. The poem was written at Camp Towanga, near Yosemite, during a weekend retreat for people who had suffered recent losses.

p. 39. At the Dog Park. Tangles. A common image used in the Zohar, a primary text of Kabbalah, to describe the clarity brought by higher consciousness or mystical insight, as in "*Mazel* [divine light or energy] releases the tangles from the higher knot, from the head of all heads." Zohar, 289a.

p. 32. Sabbath Bride. The Shekinah, or female emanation, represents God's immanence. She is said to be ready for divine marriage or symbolic reunification with God on the Sabbath. *Brucha.* Blessing.

p. 46. Heretics. The poem draws on the notion, found in a wide variety of Gnostic sects, including the medieval Cathars, that the creation of the world itself was the Fall, and that only the human mind, with its gnosis or mystical knowledge, can redeem it.

p. 48. "A kind of Divine Psychoanalysis." The title uses a phrase coined by Rabbi Burt Jacobson and refers to the practice of *Hitbodedut* in which Rabbi Nachman would go to a quiet place in the woods and pour his heart out to God, telling him whatever was on his mind

p. 49. It Hits You. Snow geese… .All listed are threatened or endangered.

p. 54. Tree of Life. In Jewish mysticism, a map of archetypes or nodes of consciousness that is based on the human body.

p. 59. A Great Blue Heron in Boynton Beach. *Tif'eret, Binah.* Sefirot, or metaphysical archetypes in Kabbalah. *Machaia.* Yiddish, a blessing of pleasure.

In This Place Where *Something's Missing* Lives

p. 64. Holy sparks, husks. In the Kabbalah of Isaac Luria, the material world is just a husk, in which sparks of the divine are hidden.

p. 70. *Ain Soph.* In Kabbalah, the first sefirot, or level of the Tree of Life, the ineffable nothingness out of which the world was created.

p. 72. Zaddik. A holy man.
Yahrtzeit candle. A memorial candle.

p. 75. Shekinah. The in-dwelling presence of God in the material world. Feminine in Hasidic thinking

p. 82. Where are you? cf. Genesis 3:9

Splendor

p.85. Title. The word "Splendor" refers to the Zohar, sometimes translated as the Book of Splendor, the primary text of Kabbalah.

p. 91 ff. All citations from the Zohar are from the translations of Daniel C. Matt, published by Stanford University Press

p. 94. Denise's Poem. "The Jacob's Ladder," from Denise Levertov's eponymous 1961 collection

P. 87. The Wedding. Wedding imagery plays an important role in Jewish mysticism, as in the wedding between the Sabbath Bride, Shekinhah, and the people of Israel that takes place each Shabbat.

p. 86. Are broken. c.f Jane Mayer, *The New Yorker,* 8/13/07

P. 90. The Other Side. *Sitra Ahra* In Kaballah, evil is viewed as an extreme domination of judgement, or *din,* over loving kindness, *hesed.*

P. 92. Confirmation Hearing. Refers to the 2018 hearings to confirm Brett Kavanaugh as Supreme Court Justice, which centered around allegations of past sexual misconduct.

P. 94. By the River of Already. The poem spins off associations from the English translation, while keeping to the spirit of loss evoked in the Zohar which refers, according to Daniel Matt, to the fact that, since the destruction of the Temple the river where Ezekial had his vision had ceased to flow.

About the Author

David Shaddock's poems have won the Ruah Magazine Power of Poetry Award for a collection of spiritual poems, and the International Peace Poem Prize, among other honors. His poems have appeared in such journals as *Tikkun, Earth First! Journal* and *Mother Jones.* His books include *In This Place Where* Something's Missing *Lives* with an afterword by Rabbi Arthur Waskow, *Dreams Are Another Set of Muscles,* with an introduction by Denise Levertov, and *Vernal Pool.* His play, "In A Company of Seekers," was performed at the 2012 Festival of Two Worlds in Spoleto, Italy. He holds a PhD in psychoanalytic research from Middlesex University London and is the author of several nonfiction books, including the forthcoming *Poetry and Psychoanalysis: The Opening of the Field.* He maintains a private psychotherapy practice in Berkeley.